A Kangaroo Mob

By Johanna Burke

Gareth Stevens
Publishing

Please visit our website, www.garethstevens.com. For a free color catalog of all our high-quality books, call toll free 1-800-542-2595 or fax 1-877-542-2596.

Library of Congress Cataloging-in-Publication Data

Burke, Johanna.
 A kangaroo mob / Johanna Burke.
    p. cm. — (Animal groups)
 Includes index.
 ISBN 978-1-4339-8200-2 (pbk.)
 ISBN 978-1-4339-8201-9 (6-pack)
 ISBN 978-1-4339-8199-9 (library binding)
 1. Kangaroos—Juvenile literature. 2. Social behavior in animals—Juvenile literature. I. Title.
 QL737.M35B866 2013
 599.2'2—dc23
                                          2012018980

First Edition

Published in 2013 by
Gareth Stevens Publishing
111 East 14th Street, Suite 349
New York, NY 10003

Copyright © 2013 Gareth Stevens Publishing

Designer: Ben Gardner
Editor: Greg Roza

Photo credits: Cover, p. 1 © iStockphoto.com/Craig Dingle; interior backgrounds Daniiel/Shutterstock.com; p. 5 Tier Und Naturfotographie J and C Sohns/Photographer's Choice/Getty Images; p. 7 (red kangaroo) Vladimir Wrangel/Shutterstock.com; p. 7 (gray kangaroo) Kitch Bain/Shutterstock.com; p. 7 (tree kangaroo) Daniel J Cox/Oxford Scientific/Getty Images; p. 9 Julie Lucht/Shutterstock.com; p. 11 Natalia Lysenko/Shutterstock.com; p. 13 Martin Mette/Shutterstock.com; p. 15 dmvphotos/Shutterstock.com; p. 17 markrhiggins/Shutterstock.com; p. 19 Jin Young Lee/ Shutterstock.com; p. 20 Sweetheart/Shutterstock.com; p. 21 Janelle Lugge/Shutterstock.com.

Printed in the United States of America

CPSIA compliance information: Batch #CW13GS: For further information contact Gareth Stevens, New York, New York at 1-800-542-2595.

Contents

Boldface words appear in the glossary.

Life in the Mob

Kangaroos are furry animals that live mostly in Australia. They have big ears. They have large back feet, and they're very good hoppers! Kangaroos live in groups called mobs. There can be more than 50 kangaroos in a mob.

Kinds of Kangaroos

There are many kinds of kangaroos. Red kangaroos are the largest kind. They can be as tall as an adult person. Gray kangaroos are the most common kind. Tree kangaroos live in trees! All kinds live in mobs.

red kangaroo

gray kangaroo

tree kangaroo

7

Mob Members

Male kangaroos are called boomers. A mob has one male leader. Sometimes other males live in a mob, too. Females are called flyers. They care for young kangaroos. Young kangaroos are called joeys. Joeys love to play.

Roo Range

Kangaroos eat at night and rest during the day. They eat grass and leaves. Kangaroos drink water whenever they can find it. A mob will travel far away from their home **range** to find food, but they often come back.

11

Safety in the Mob

Mobs keep kangaroos safe. Some kangaroos watch for enemies, such as **dingoes**, while the others eat or sleep. When an enemy is near, a kangaroo stomps its feet. This warns the rest of the mob of **danger**.

13

Talking with Kangaroos

The kangaroos in a mob **communicate** in many ways. They grunt, cough, and hiss. They growl when they're mad. Mothers make a clicking sound to call their joeys. Kangaroos also **groom** new mob members to learn about them.

15

Growing Up

Female kangaroos have pouches. This is where newborn joeys live. As a joey gets bigger, it climbs in and out of the pouch. A mother often has a joey in her pouch and an older joey by her side.

Adult Kangaroos

Female kangaroos often stay with their mothers even after they have their own joeys. When boomers grow up, they might leave the mob to join a new one. Or they might start a mob of their own.

Boxing Boomers

Kangaroos love living in a mob. They get along most of the time. When boomers get angry, they "box." They kick each other with their feet. Joeys and flyers box, too. But they're just having fun!

Fun Facts About Kangaroos

Kangaroos can't walk backwards, but they're very good swimmers.

Depending on the kind, kangaroos can live between 7 and 18 years.

The smallest kangaroo is the musky rat kangaroo. It's only about 8 inches (20 cm) tall.

Red kangaroos can cover 15 feet (4.6 m) with one hop!

Glossary

communicate: to share ideas and feelings through sounds and motions

danger: something that can cause harm

dingo: a wild Australian dog with a reddish-brown coat

groom: to clean

range: the area where something lives

For More Information

Books

Riggs, Kate. *Kangaroos*. Mankato, MN: Creative Education, 2012.

Robbins, Lynette. *Kangaroos*. New York, NY: PowerKids Press, 2012.

Wood, Jenny. *I Wonder Why Kangaroos Have Pouches*. Boston, MA: Kingfisher, 2011.

Websites

Animal Bytes: Kangaroo and Wallaby
www.sandiegozoo.org/animalbytes/t-kangaroo.html
Learn more about kangaroos and their close cousins, wallabies.

Kangaroos
kids.nationalgeographic.com/kids/animals/creaturefeature/kangaroos
Read more about kangaroos and see pictures of them.

Index